50 Greek Platter Recipes for Home

By: Kelly Johnson

Table of Contents

- Spanakopita (Spinach Pie)
- Moussaka
- Souvlaki (Grilled Meat Skewers)
- Tzatziki
- Dolmades (Stuffed Grape Leaves)
- Greek Salad
- Gyro Platter
- Tiropita (Cheese Pie)
- Pastitsio
- Feta Cheese with Olives and Herbs
- Keftedes (Greek Meatballs)
- Baklava
- Saganaki (Fried Cheese)
- Greek Chicken Souvlaki Platter
- Grilled Octopus
- Stifado (Greek Beef Stew)
- Greek Lemon Potatoes
- Pita Bread with Hummus and Olive Tapenade
- Yemista (Stuffed Vegetables)
- Greek Yogurt with Honey and Nuts
- Grilled Halloumi Cheese with Watermelon
- Koulouri (Greek Sesame Bread Rings)
- Galaktoboureko (Custard Pie)
- Gemista (Stuffed Bell Peppers)
- Greek Fava Bean Dip
- Kolokythokeftedes (Zucchini Fritters)
- Keftethes (Greek Meatballs)
- Garides Saganaki (Shrimp in Tomato Sauce with Feta)
- Greek Lamb Chops with Tzatziki
- Revithia (Greek Chickpea Soup)
- Melitzanosalata (Greek Eggplant Dip)
- Pita Bread with Greek Salad Filling
- Psarosoupa (Greek Fish Soup)
- Greek Orzo Salad
- Tyropita (Feta Cheese Pie)

- Greek Spinach and Feta Stuffed Chicken
- Kalamata Olive Tapenade
- Octopus Salad
- Greek Spinach Rice (Spanakorizo)
- Melomakarona (Greek Honey Cookies)
- Greek-style Stuffed Mushrooms
- Gigantes Plaki (Baked Giant Beans)
- Greek-style Roasted Leg of Lamb
- Lahanodolmades (Cabbage Rolls)
- Kolokithopita (Savory Zucchini Pie)
- Greek-style Roasted Vegetables
- Pita Bread with Greek Yogurt and Cucumber
- Grilled Calamari
- Greek-style Grilled Eggplant
- Loukoumades (Greek Honey Puffs)

Spanakopita (Spinach Pie)

Ingredients:

For the filling:

- 1 kg fresh spinach, washed and chopped
- 200g feta cheese, crumbled
- 1 onion, finely chopped
- 3-4 spring onions, finely chopped
- 2-3 cloves garlic, minced
- 1/2 cup fresh dill, chopped
- 1/4 cup fresh parsley, chopped
- Salt and pepper to taste
- Olive oil for sautéing

For the pastry:

- 1 package (about 400g) phyllo pastry sheets, thawed if frozen
- 1/2 cup melted butter or olive oil for brushing

Instructions:

1. Preheat your oven to 180°C (350°F).
2. In a large skillet, heat some olive oil over medium heat. Add the chopped onion and spring onions, and sauté until softened, about 3-4 minutes. Add the minced garlic and cook for another minute.
3. Add the chopped spinach to the skillet in batches, stirring until wilted. Cook for about 5-7 minutes until the excess moisture evaporates. Remove from heat and let it cool slightly.
4. Transfer the cooked spinach mixture to a large bowl. Add crumbled feta cheese, chopped dill, parsley, salt, and pepper. Mix well until all ingredients are evenly distributed.
5. Brush a baking dish with olive oil or melted butter. Lay one sheet of phyllo pastry in the dish, allowing the edges to hang over the sides. Brush the phyllo sheet

lightly with melted butter or olive oil. Repeat with several more sheets, layering them and brushing each one with butter or oil.
6. Spread the spinach and feta filling evenly over the layered phyllo sheets.
7. Fold the overhanging edges of the phyllo pastry over the filling, then layer more phyllo sheets on top, brushing each one with butter or oil as before.
8. Once you've used all the filling and phyllo sheets, brush the top layer generously with butter or oil.
9. Using a sharp knife, score the top of the pie into squares or triangles, being careful not to cut all the way through.
10. Bake in the preheated oven for 45-50 minutes, or until the phyllo pastry is golden brown and crispy.
11. Allow the spanakopita to cool for a few minutes before slicing and serving. Enjoy this delicious Greek spinach pie warm or at room temperature!

Spanakopita is a versatile dish that can be served as a main course or as part of a mezze platter. It's perfect for any occasion and is sure to be a hit with family and friends.

Moussaka

Ingredients:

For the moussaka layers:

- 2 large eggplants, sliced lengthwise into 1/2-inch thick slices
- Salt, for sweating the eggplant
- Olive oil, for brushing the eggplant
- 500g minced lamb or beef
- 1 onion, finely chopped
- 3 cloves garlic, minced
- 1 can (400g) crushed tomatoes
- 1 teaspoon dried oregano
- 1 teaspoon dried thyme
- Salt and pepper, to taste
- Pinch of cinnamon (optional)

For the béchamel sauce:

- 50g butter
- 1/3 cup all-purpose flour
- 2 cups milk
- Salt and pepper, to taste
- Pinch of nutmeg

Instructions:

1. Preheat your oven to 200°C (400°F).
2. Place the eggplant slices in a colander and sprinkle them generously with salt. Let them sit for about 30 minutes to draw out any bitterness. After 30 minutes, rinse the eggplant slices under cold water and pat them dry with paper towels.
3. Arrange the eggplant slices in a single layer on baking trays lined with parchment paper. Brush both sides of the eggplant slices with olive oil. Bake in the

preheated oven for about 20-25 minutes, or until they are tender and lightly browned. Remove from the oven and set aside.
4. While the eggplant is baking, prepare the meat sauce. In a large skillet, heat some olive oil over medium heat. Add the chopped onion and cook until softened, about 5 minutes. Add the minced garlic and cook for another minute.
5. Add the minced lamb or beef to the skillet, breaking it up with a spoon, and cook until browned.
6. Stir in the crushed tomatoes, dried oregano, dried thyme, salt, pepper, and cinnamon (if using). Simmer the sauce for about 15-20 minutes, or until it has thickened slightly. Remove from heat and set aside.
7. To make the béchamel sauce, melt the butter in a saucepan over medium heat. Once melted, add the flour and whisk continuously for 1-2 minutes to cook out the raw flour taste.
8. Gradually pour in the milk, whisking constantly to prevent lumps from forming. Cook the sauce until it thickens and coats the back of a spoon. Season with salt, pepper, and nutmeg to taste. Remove from heat and set aside.
9. To assemble the moussaka, spread half of the eggplant slices in the bottom of a greased baking dish. Top with half of the meat sauce, spreading it evenly over the eggplant.
10. Layer the remaining eggplant slices on top of the meat sauce, followed by the remaining meat sauce.
11. Pour the béchamel sauce over the top of the moussaka, spreading it evenly with a spatula.
12. Bake the moussaka in the preheated oven for 45-50 minutes, or until the top is golden brown and bubbly.
13. Allow the moussaka to cool for a few minutes before slicing and serving. Enjoy this hearty and comforting Greek dish with a side of salad and crusty bread!

Moussaka is a labor of love, but the end result is absolutely worth it. It's a delicious and satisfying dish that's perfect for sharing with family and friends.

Souvlaki (Grilled Meat Skewers)

Ingredients:

For the marinade:

- 500g boneless lamb, beef, or chicken, cut into 1-inch cubes
- 1/4 cup olive oil
- 3 cloves garlic, minced
- 2 tablespoons lemon juice
- 1 teaspoon dried oregano
- 1 teaspoon dried thyme
- 1 teaspoon paprika
- 1/2 teaspoon cumin
- Salt and pepper, to taste

For serving:

- Pita bread
- Tzatziki sauce
- Chopped tomatoes
- Chopped cucumbers
- Chopped red onion
- Chopped fresh parsley
- Lemon wedges

Instructions:

1. In a large bowl, combine the olive oil, minced garlic, lemon juice, dried oregano, dried thyme, paprika, cumin, salt, and pepper to make the marinade.
2. Add the cubed meat to the marinade, making sure it is evenly coated. Cover the bowl and refrigerate for at least 1 hour, or overnight for best results.
3. If you're using wooden skewers, soak them in water for at least 30 minutes to prevent them from burning on the grill.
4. Preheat your grill to medium-high heat.

5. Thread the marinated meat onto the skewers, leaving a little space between each piece.
6. Grill the skewers for about 8-10 minutes, turning occasionally, until the meat is cooked through and slightly charred on the outside.
7. While the meat is grilling, warm the pita bread on the grill for a minute or so on each side, until it's warm and slightly toasted.
8. Serve the grilled souvlaki skewers on warm pita bread, topped with tzatziki sauce, chopped tomatoes, cucumbers, red onion, and fresh parsley. Squeeze some lemon juice over the top for extra flavor.
9. Roll up the pita bread around the souvlaki skewers and toppings to form a wrap, or serve them open-faced on a plate.
10. Enjoy your homemade souvlaki with all the traditional Greek fixings for a delicious and satisfying meal!

Souvlaki is a versatile dish that's perfect for summer grilling or indoor cooking year-round. Whether you're making it for a casual dinner or a festive gathering, it's sure to be a hit with family and friends.

Tzatziki

Ingredients:

- 1 English cucumber, grated
- 2 cups Greek yogurt (or strained regular yogurt)
- 2 cloves garlic, minced
- 2 tablespoons extra virgin olive oil
- 1 tablespoon fresh lemon juice
- 1 tablespoon chopped fresh dill (or mint)
- Salt and pepper, to taste

Instructions:

1. Start by grating the cucumber using a box grater or food processor. Once grated, place the cucumber in a fine-mesh sieve or colander over a bowl. Sprinkle with a little salt and let it sit for about 10-15 minutes to release excess moisture.
2. While the cucumber is draining, prepare the yogurt mixture. In a mixing bowl, combine the Greek yogurt, minced garlic, olive oil, lemon juice, and chopped fresh dill. Stir well to combine.
3. After the cucumber has drained, use your hands or a clean kitchen towel to squeeze out any remaining liquid. Add the grated cucumber to the yogurt mixture and mix until well combined.
4. Taste the tzatziki and adjust the seasoning with salt and pepper, if needed.
5. Cover the tzatziki and refrigerate for at least 1 hour to allow the flavors to meld together.
6. Before serving, give the tzatziki a good stir. If it has thickened too much in the fridge, you can thin it out with a little water or more lemon juice.
7. Serve the tzatziki as a sauce alongside grilled meats, gyros, or souvlaki. It's also delicious as a dip for pita bread, vegetables, or crackers.
8. Enjoy the cool and creamy goodness of homemade tzatziki!

Tzatziki is a versatile condiment that adds a burst of flavor to any dish. Feel free to adjust the ingredients to suit your taste preferences, adding more garlic, lemon juice, or herbs as desired.

Dolmades (Stuffed Grape Leaves)

Ingredients:

For the grape leaves:

- 1 jar of preserved grape leaves (about 60-70 leaves)
- Water, for soaking the grape leaves
- Salt, for seasoning the water

For the filling:

- 1 cup short-grain rice (such as Arborio or sushi rice)
- 1 large onion, finely chopped
- 2-3 cloves garlic, minced
- 1/4 cup extra virgin olive oil
- 1/4 cup fresh dill, chopped
- 1/4 cup fresh mint, chopped
- 1/4 cup fresh parsley, chopped
- 1/4 cup pine nuts, toasted
- 1/4 cup currants or raisins (optional)
- Salt and pepper, to taste
- Juice of 1-2 lemons

For cooking:

- Water or vegetable broth, for boiling
- Extra virgin olive oil, for drizzling
- Lemon wedges, for serving

Instructions:

1. Start by preparing the grape leaves. If using preserved grape leaves, remove them from the jar and rinse them thoroughly under cold water to remove any excess

salt or brine. Place the grape leaves in a large bowl and cover them with hot water. Let them soak for about 10-15 minutes to soften. After soaking, drain the grape leaves and pat them dry with paper towels.

2. While the grape leaves are soaking, prepare the filling. In a large skillet, heat the olive oil over medium heat. Add the chopped onion and cook until softened, about 5 minutes. Add the minced garlic and cook for another minute.
3. Stir in the rice and cook for a few minutes, stirring frequently, until the rice is lightly toasted.
4. Add the chopped herbs (dill, mint, and parsley), toasted pine nuts, and currants or raisins (if using) to the skillet. Season with salt and pepper to taste. Stir well to combine all the ingredients.
5. Remove the skillet from the heat and let the filling cool slightly.
6. To assemble the dolmades, place a grape leaf shiny side down on a clean work surface. Trim off any tough stems with kitchen shears.
7. Place about a tablespoon of the filling near the stem end of the grape leaf. Fold the bottom of the leaf over the filling, then fold in the sides, and roll it up tightly into a little bundle.
8. Repeat the process with the remaining grape leaves and filling, arranging the dolmades in a single layer in a large pot or Dutch oven.
9. Once all the dolmades are assembled, pour enough water or vegetable broth over them to cover. Place a heavy plate or lid on top of the dolmades to keep them submerged in the liquid.
10. Bring the pot to a boil over medium-high heat, then reduce the heat to low and simmer gently for about 45-60 minutes, or until the rice is cooked and the grape leaves are tender.
11. Once cooked, carefully remove the dolmades from the pot using a slotted spoon and arrange them on a serving platter.
12. Drizzle the dolmades with extra virgin olive oil and squeeze fresh lemon juice over the top.
13. Serve the dolmades warm or at room temperature, with extra lemon wedges on the side.

Enjoy these delicious and flavorful stuffed grape leaves as a appetizer or part of a mezze spread! They're perfect for sharing with family and friends at any gathering.

Greek Salad

Ingredients:

For the salad:

- 2 large ripe tomatoes, cut into wedges
- 1 cucumber, thinly sliced
- 1 red onion, thinly sliced
- 1 green bell pepper, thinly sliced
- 1/2 cup Kalamata olives, pitted
- 200g feta cheese, crumbled
- Handful of fresh oregano leaves (optional)
- Salt and pepper, to taste

For the dressing:

- 1/4 cup extra virgin olive oil
- 2 tablespoons red wine vinegar
- 1 clove garlic, minced
- 1 teaspoon dried oregano
- Salt and pepper, to taste

Instructions:

1. In a large salad bowl, combine the tomato wedges, sliced cucumber, sliced red onion, sliced bell pepper, and Kalamata olives.
2. Season the salad with salt and pepper to taste, and toss gently to combine.
3. In a small bowl or jar, whisk together the olive oil, red wine vinegar, minced garlic, dried oregano, salt, and pepper to make the dressing.
4. Pour the dressing over the salad and toss gently to coat the vegetables evenly.
5. Sprinkle the crumbled feta cheese over the top of the salad.
6. If using, garnish the salad with fresh oregano leaves for an extra burst of flavor.
7. Serve the Greek salad immediately as a side dish or as a light and refreshing main course.

8. Enjoy this vibrant and flavorful salad with crusty bread or alongside grilled meats or seafood for a delicious Greek-inspired meal!

Greek salad is simple to make and bursting with fresh flavors. Feel free to customize it with your favorite vegetables or add-ons, such as cherry tomatoes, avocado, or grilled artichoke hearts. It's a versatile dish that's perfect for any occasion!

Gyro Platter

Ingredients:

For the gyro meat:

- 500g boneless lamb, chicken, or beef, thinly sliced
- 2 tablespoons olive oil
- 3 cloves garlic, minced
- 1 teaspoon dried oregano
- 1 teaspoon dried thyme
- 1 teaspoon paprika
- 1/2 teaspoon cumin
- Salt and pepper, to taste

For serving:

- Pita bread
- Tzatziki sauce (see previous recipe)
- Chopped tomatoes
- Chopped cucumbers
- Sliced red onion
- Chopped fresh parsley
- Lemon wedges

Instructions:

1. In a bowl, combine the olive oil, minced garlic, dried oregano, dried thyme, paprika, cumin, salt, and pepper to make the marinade for the gyro meat.
2. Add the thinly sliced meat to the marinade, making sure it is evenly coated. Cover the bowl and refrigerate for at least 1 hour, or overnight for best results.
3. Preheat your grill or skillet to medium-high heat.
4. Thread the marinated meat onto skewers or place it directly on the grill or skillet. Cook the meat for about 3-4 minutes on each side, or until cooked through and nicely charred.

5. While the meat is cooking, warm the pita bread on the grill or in a skillet for a minute or so on each side, until it's warm and slightly toasted.
6. Once the meat is cooked, remove it from the grill or skillet and let it rest for a few minutes. Then, thinly slice the meat against the grain.
7. To assemble the gyro platter, arrange the sliced meat on a serving platter, along with warmed pita bread.
8. Serve the gyro platter with tzatziki sauce, chopped tomatoes, chopped cucumbers, sliced red onion, chopped fresh parsley, and lemon wedges on the side.
9. Allow everyone to assemble their own gyro sandwiches by filling the pita bread with the sliced meat and desired toppings, and drizzling with tzatziki sauce.
10. Enjoy this delicious and flavorful gyro platter as a hearty meal or as part of a Mediterranean-inspired feast!

Gyro platters are perfect for casual dinners or gatherings with family and friends.

They're easy to customize with your favorite toppings and are sure to be a hit with everyone at the table.

Tiropita (Cheese Pie)

Ingredients:

- 1 package phyllo dough, thawed according to package instructions
- 1/2 cup unsalted butter, melted
- 2 cups feta cheese, crumbled
- 1 cup ricotta cheese
- 2 eggs, lightly beaten
- 1/4 cup chopped fresh parsley
- Salt and pepper, to taste

Instructions:

1. Preheat your oven to 350°F (175°C). Grease a 9x13-inch baking dish with butter or cooking spray.
2. In a mixing bowl, combine the crumbled feta cheese, ricotta cheese, beaten eggs, chopped parsley, salt, and pepper. Mix until well combined.
3. Lay a sheet of phyllo dough in the prepared baking dish and brush it with melted butter. Repeat with several more sheets of phyllo dough, brushing each layer with butter as you go, until you have a few layers on the bottom of the dish.
4. Spread the cheese filling evenly over the phyllo dough layers in the baking dish.
5. Continue layering phyllo dough sheets on top of the cheese filling, brushing each sheet with melted butter, until you have used up all the phyllo dough.
6. Using a sharp knife, score the tiropita into squares or triangles, being careful not to cut all the way through the bottom.
7. Bake in the preheated oven for 45-50 minutes, or until the phyllo dough is golden brown and crispy.
8. Remove the tiropita from the oven and let it cool for a few minutes before serving.

Tiropita is best served warm or at room temperature. It makes a delicious appetizer, snack, or side dish for any occasion. Enjoy!

Pastitsio

Ingredients:

For the meat sauce:

- 1 pound ground beef or lamb
- 1 onion, finely chopped
- 2 cloves garlic, minced
- 1 can (14 ounces) crushed tomatoes
- 1/4 cup tomato paste
- 1/2 cup red wine (optional)
- 1 teaspoon dried oregano
- 1 teaspoon dried mint
- Salt and pepper, to taste
- 1 tablespoon olive oil

For the béchamel sauce:

- 4 cups milk
- 1/2 cup unsalted butter
- 1/2 cup all-purpose flour
- 1/4 teaspoon ground nutmeg
- Salt and pepper, to taste
- 2 eggs, lightly beaten
- 1 cup grated Parmesan cheese

For the pasta:

- 1 pound penne or other tubular pasta
- Salt, for boiling

Instructions:

1. Preheat your oven to 350°F (175°C). Grease a 9x13-inch baking dish with butter or cooking spray.
2. Cook the pasta in a large pot of salted boiling water according to the package instructions until al dente. Drain and set aside.
3. To make the meat sauce, heat olive oil in a large skillet over medium heat. Add the chopped onion and minced garlic, and cook until softened, about 5 minutes.
4. Add the ground beef or lamb to the skillet and cook until browned, breaking it up with a spoon as it cooks.
5. Stir in the crushed tomatoes, tomato paste, red wine (if using), dried oregano, dried mint, salt, and pepper. Simmer the sauce for about 15-20 minutes, until thickened. Remove from heat and set aside.
6. To make the béchamel sauce, melt the butter in a saucepan over medium heat. Stir in the flour and cook, stirring constantly, for about 2 minutes to make a roux.
7. Gradually whisk in the milk, a little at a time, until smooth. Cook the sauce, stirring constantly, until it thickens and comes to a simmer.
8. Remove the béchamel sauce from heat and stir in the ground nutmeg, salt, and pepper. Let it cool slightly, then gradually whisk in the beaten eggs and grated Parmesan cheese.
9. To assemble the pastitsio, spread half of the cooked pasta in the bottom of the prepared baking dish. Top with the meat sauce, spreading it evenly over the pasta.
10. Layer the remaining pasta on top of the meat sauce, then pour the béchamel sauce over the pasta, spreading it out evenly to cover the top.
11. Bake the pastitsio in the preheated oven for 45-50 minutes, or until the top is golden brown and bubbling.
12. Remove from the oven and let it cool for a few minutes before slicing and serving.

Pastitsio is a comforting and hearty dish that's perfect for serving at family gatherings or special occasions. Enjoy!

Feta Cheese with Olives and Herbs

Ingredients:

- 8 ounces feta cheese, block or crumbled
- 1/2 cup mixed olives, pitted
- 2 tablespoons extra virgin olive oil
- 1 tablespoon fresh herbs (such as oregano, thyme, or rosemary), chopped
- Zest of 1 lemon (optional)
- Freshly ground black pepper, to taste

Instructions:

1. Arrange the block of feta cheese in the center of a serving platter or shallow dish. If using crumbled feta, simply spread it evenly over the bottom of the dish.
2. Scatter the mixed olives around the feta cheese, arranging them in an attractive pattern.
3. Drizzle the extra virgin olive oil over the feta cheese and olives, ensuring they are evenly coated.
4. Sprinkle the chopped fresh herbs over the top of the feta cheese and olives, distributing them evenly.
5. If desired, sprinkle the lemon zest over the dish for an extra burst of flavor.
6. Finish with a few twists of freshly ground black pepper to taste.
7. Serve the feta cheese with olives and herbs immediately, accompanied by crusty bread or crackers for dipping.

This feta cheese with olives and herbs is perfect for serving as part of a mezze platter, appetizer spread, or as a light and flavorful snack. It's a versatile dish that's sure to impress your guests with its vibrant colors and bold flavors. Enjoy!

Keftedes (Greek Meatballs)

Ingredients:

- 1 pound ground beef or lamb
- 1 small onion, grated
- 2 cloves garlic, minced
- 1/4 cup fresh parsley, finely chopped
- 1/4 cup fresh mint, finely chopped
- 1/2 cup breadcrumbs
- 1 egg, lightly beaten
- 1 teaspoon dried oregano
- 1/2 teaspoon ground cumin
- Salt and pepper, to taste
- Olive oil, for frying

Instructions:

1. In a large mixing bowl, combine the ground beef or lamb, grated onion, minced garlic, chopped parsley, chopped mint, breadcrumbs, beaten egg, dried oregano, ground cumin, salt, and pepper. Mix until all the ingredients are well combined.
2. Shape the meat mixture into small meatballs, about 1 inch in diameter, and place them on a plate or baking sheet lined with parchment paper.
3. Heat a few tablespoons of olive oil in a large skillet over medium heat.
4. Once the oil is hot, add the meatballs to the skillet in batches, making sure not to overcrowd the pan. Cook the meatballs for 3-4 minutes on each side, or until they are browned and cooked through.
5. Remove the cooked meatballs from the skillet and place them on a plate lined with paper towels to drain any excess oil.
6. Repeat the process with the remaining meatballs, adding more oil to the skillet as needed.
7. Serve the keftedes hot, garnished with additional fresh herbs if desired, and accompanied by tzatziki sauce or lemon wedges for dipping.

These Greek meatballs are perfect for serving as an appetizer, side dish, or main course. They're juicy, flavorful, and aromatic, with a delicious blend of herbs and spices that will transport you to the sunny shores of Greece with every bite. Enjoy!

Baklava

Ingredients:

- 1 package (16 ounces) phyllo dough, thawed according to package instructions
- 1 cup unsalted butter, melted
- 2 cups mixed nuts (such as walnuts, almonds, and pistachios), finely chopped
- 1/2 cup granulated sugar
- 1 teaspoon ground cinnamon
- 1/4 teaspoon ground cloves
- 1 cup water
- 1 cup granulated sugar
- 1/2 cup honey
- 1 tablespoon lemon juice
- 1 teaspoon vanilla extract

Instructions:

1. Preheat your oven to 350°F (175°C). Grease a 9x13-inch baking dish with butter or cooking spray.
2. In a mixing bowl, combine the finely chopped nuts, 1/2 cup granulated sugar, ground cinnamon, and ground cloves. Mix until well combined and set aside.
3. Unroll the phyllo dough and cover it with a damp kitchen towel to prevent it from drying out.
4. Place one sheet of phyllo dough in the prepared baking dish and brush it with melted butter. Repeat with several more sheets of phyllo dough, brushing each layer with butter as you go, until you have about 10 sheets on the bottom of the dish.
5. Sprinkle a thin layer of the nut mixture evenly over the top of the phyllo dough.
6. Continue layering phyllo dough sheets on top of the nut mixture, brushing each sheet with butter, until you have used about half of the phyllo dough.
7. Sprinkle another layer of the nut mixture over the top of the phyllo dough.
8. Continue layering the remaining phyllo dough sheets on top of the nut mixture, brushing each sheet with butter, until you have used all of the phyllo dough.
9. Using a sharp knife, carefully cut the baklava into diamond or square-shaped pieces.
10. Bake the baklava in the preheated oven for 45-50 minutes, or until the top is golden brown and crisp.

11. While the baklava is baking, prepare the syrup. In a saucepan, combine the water, 1 cup granulated sugar, honey, lemon juice, and vanilla extract. Bring the mixture to a boil over medium heat, then reduce the heat to low and simmer for 10 minutes.
12. Remove the baklava from the oven and immediately pour the hot syrup over the hot baklava, making sure to cover all the pieces evenly.
13. Let the baklava cool completely in the baking dish before serving.

Baklava is best served at room temperature and can be stored in an airtight container at room temperature for several days. Enjoy this sweet and nutty dessert as a delightful ending to any meal or as a special treat for celebrations and gatherings.

Saganaki (Fried Cheese)

Ingredients:

- 8 ounces Kefalograviera cheese or Kasseri cheese, sliced into 1/2-inch thick pieces
- 1/4 cup all-purpose flour
- 1/4 teaspoon paprika
- 1/4 teaspoon dried oregano
- Pinch of salt
- Pinch of black pepper
- 2 tablespoons olive oil
- 1 tablespoon brandy or ouzo (optional)
- 1 lemon, cut into wedges, for serving
- Chopped fresh parsley, for garnish (optional)

Instructions:

1. In a shallow dish, combine the all-purpose flour, paprika, dried oregano, salt, and black pepper. Mix until well combined.
2. Dredge the slices of cheese in the seasoned flour mixture, shaking off any excess flour.
3. Heat the olive oil in a large skillet over medium-high heat.
4. Once the oil is hot, add the cheese slices to the skillet in a single layer, being careful not to overcrowd the pan. You may need to cook the cheese slices in batches.
5. Fry the cheese slices for 1-2 minutes on each side, or until golden brown and crispy.
6. If using, carefully pour the brandy or ouzo over the cheese in the skillet and allow it to ignite. Let the flames burn out on their own.
7. Remove the fried cheese from the skillet and transfer it to a serving plate.
8. Garnish the saganaki with chopped fresh parsley, if desired, and serve immediately with lemon wedges on the side.

Saganaki is best served hot and crispy, with a squeeze of lemon juice over the top. Enjoy this delicious Greek appetizer as part of a meze spread or as a starter for any meal. It's sure to be a hit with cheese lovers!

Greek Chicken Souvlaki Platter

Ingredients:

For the Chicken Souvlaki:

- 1 ½ pounds boneless, skinless chicken breasts, cut into bite-sized pieces
- ¼ cup olive oil
- ¼ cup lemon juice
- 3 cloves garlic, minced
- 1 teaspoon dried oregano
- 1 teaspoon dried thyme
- 1 teaspoon paprika
- Salt and pepper, to taste
- Wooden skewers, soaked in water for at least 30 minutes

For the Tzatziki Sauce:

- 1 cup Greek yogurt
- 1 cucumber, grated and squeezed to remove excess moisture
- 2 cloves garlic, minced
- 1 tablespoon lemon juice
- 1 tablespoon extra virgin olive oil
- 1 tablespoon chopped fresh dill (optional)
- Salt and pepper, to taste

For Serving:

- Pita bread or flatbread
- Sliced tomatoes
- Sliced red onions
- Sliced cucumbers
- Kalamata olives
- Feta cheese, crumbled
- Lemon wedges

- Chopped fresh parsley, for garnish

Instructions:

1. In a bowl, combine the olive oil, lemon juice, minced garlic, dried oregano, dried thyme, paprika, salt, and pepper to make the marinade for the chicken souvlaki.
2. Add the chicken pieces to the marinade and toss to coat. Cover the bowl and refrigerate for at least 1 hour, or overnight for best results.
3. While the chicken is marinating, prepare the tzatziki sauce. In another bowl, combine the Greek yogurt, grated cucumber, minced garlic, lemon juice, extra virgin olive oil, chopped fresh dill (if using), salt, and pepper. Mix well, then cover and refrigerate until ready to serve.
4. Preheat your grill or grill pan to medium-high heat.
5. Thread the marinated chicken pieces onto the soaked wooden skewers.
6. Grill the chicken skewers for 4-5 minutes per side, or until cooked through and lightly charred.
7. Once the chicken is cooked, remove it from the grill and let it rest for a few minutes.
8. To assemble the platter, arrange the grilled chicken skewers on a large serving platter.
9. Serve the chicken souvlaki with pita bread or flatbread, sliced tomatoes, sliced red onions, sliced cucumbers, Kalamata olives, crumbled feta cheese, lemon wedges, and tzatziki sauce.
10. Garnish the platter with chopped fresh parsley for a pop of color and freshness.
11. Serve immediately and enjoy!

This Greek Chicken Souvlaki Platter is perfect for a casual gathering or a special meal with family and friends. It's packed with flavor and offers a variety of textures and tastes that will delight your taste buds. Enjoy this taste of Greece!

Grilled Octopus

Ingredients:

- 2 pounds octopus (fresh or frozen), cleaned and tentacles separated
- 1/4 cup extra virgin olive oil
- 4 cloves garlic, minced
- 2 tablespoons fresh lemon juice
- 1 teaspoon dried oregano
- Salt and pepper, to taste
- Lemon wedges, for serving
- Chopped fresh parsley, for garnish

Instructions:

1. If using frozen octopus, make sure it is fully thawed before cooking. Rinse the octopus under cold water and pat it dry with paper towels.
2. In a large pot of boiling water, blanch the octopus for about 3-4 minutes. This helps to tenderize the octopus and prepares it for grilling.
3. Remove the octopus from the boiling water and let it cool slightly. Pat it dry with paper towels to remove excess moisture.
4. In a bowl, whisk together the extra virgin olive oil, minced garlic, fresh lemon juice, dried oregano, salt, and pepper to make the marinade.
5. Place the octopus in a shallow dish or resealable plastic bag, and pour the marinade over it. Make sure the octopus is evenly coated in the marinade. Cover the dish or seal the bag, and let the octopus marinate in the refrigerator for at least 1 hour, or overnight for best results.
6. Preheat your grill to medium-high heat.
7. Remove the octopus from the marinade and discard any excess marinade.
8. Grill the octopus for about 2-3 minutes per side, or until it is lightly charred and heated through.
9. Once the octopus is grilled to perfection, remove it from the grill and transfer it to a serving platter.
10. Serve the grilled octopus hot, garnished with lemon wedges and chopped fresh parsley.

Grilled octopus is best enjoyed immediately, while it's still warm and tender. It pairs well with a squeeze of fresh lemon juice and a sprinkle of chopped parsley for added freshness. Serve it as an appetizer or as part of a seafood feast for a memorable dining experience. Enjoy!

Stifado (Greek Beef Stew)

Ingredients:

- 2 pounds beef stew meat, cut into cubes
- 2 tablespoons olive oil
- 2 onions, thinly sliced
- 4 cloves garlic, minced
- 2 tablespoons tomato paste
- 1 cup beef broth
- 1 cup red wine
- 1/4 cup red wine vinegar
- 1 cinnamon stick
- 4 cloves
- 2 bay leaves
- 1 teaspoon dried oregano
- 1 teaspoon dried thyme
- Salt and pepper, to taste
- 1 pound small onions or pearl onions, peeled
- 1 pound baby potatoes, halved
- Chopped fresh parsley, for garnish

Instructions:

1. In a large pot or Dutch oven, heat the olive oil over medium heat. Add the beef stew meat and cook until browned on all sides. Remove the beef from the pot and set aside.
2. In the same pot, add the sliced onions and minced garlic. Cook until the onions are soft and translucent, about 5 minutes.
3. Stir in the tomato paste and cook for an additional 2 minutes.
4. Return the browned beef to the pot and add the beef broth, red wine, red wine vinegar, cinnamon stick, cloves, bay leaves, dried oregano, dried thyme, salt, and pepper. Stir to combine.
5. Bring the mixture to a boil, then reduce the heat to low. Cover the pot and simmer for 1 hour, stirring occasionally.
6. After 1 hour, add the peeled onions and halved baby potatoes to the pot. Stir to combine.

7. Cover the pot again and continue to simmer for an additional 45 minutes to 1 hour, or until the beef is tender and the onions and potatoes are cooked through.
8. Once the stew is ready, remove the cinnamon stick, cloves, and bay leaves from the pot.
9. Taste and adjust the seasoning with salt and pepper, if needed.
10. Serve the stifado hot, garnished with chopped fresh parsley.

Stifado is often served with crusty bread or over a bed of rice or mashed potatoes to soak up the delicious sauce. It's a comforting and satisfying dish that's perfect for cooler weather or any time you're craving a hearty meal. Enjoy!

Greek Lemon Potatoes

Ingredients:

- 4 large potatoes, peeled and cut into wedges
- 1/3 cup extra virgin olive oil
- 1/4 cup fresh lemon juice
- 3 cloves garlic, minced
- 1 teaspoon dried oregano
- 1 teaspoon dried thyme
- 1 teaspoon dried rosemary
- Salt and pepper, to taste
- 1 cup chicken or vegetable broth
- 1/4 cup water
- Fresh parsley, chopped, for garnish
- Lemon wedges, for serving

Instructions:

1. Preheat your oven to 400°F (200°C).
2. In a large bowl, combine the olive oil, lemon juice, minced garlic, dried oregano, dried thyme, dried rosemary, salt, and pepper. Whisk until well combined.
3. Add the potato wedges to the bowl and toss to coat them evenly with the lemon and herb mixture.
4. Transfer the potatoes to a baking dish or sheet pan, arranging them in a single layer.
5. Pour the chicken or vegetable broth and water over the potatoes in the baking dish.
6. Cover the baking dish with aluminum foil and bake in the preheated oven for 30 minutes.
7. After 30 minutes, remove the aluminum foil from the baking dish and return it to the oven.
8. Continue baking the potatoes, uncovered, for an additional 30-40 minutes, or until they are golden brown and crispy on the outside, and tender on the inside. Be sure to turn the potatoes halfway through the cooking time to ensure even browning.

9. Once the potatoes are done, remove them from the oven and transfer them to a serving platter.
10. Garnish the potatoes with chopped fresh parsley and serve hot, with lemon wedges on the side for squeezing over the top.

These Greek lemon potatoes are bursting with flavor from the tangy lemon juice and aromatic herbs. They make a delicious side dish for roasted meats, grilled fish, or as part of a vegetarian meal. Enjoy!

Pita Bread with Hummus and Olive Tapenade

Ingredients:

For the Hummus:

- 1 can (15 ounces) chickpeas, drained and rinsed
- 2 cloves garlic, minced
- 1/4 cup tahini
- 3 tablespoons lemon juice
- 2 tablespoons extra virgin olive oil
- 1/2 teaspoon ground cumin
- Salt, to taste
- Water, as needed

For the Olive Tapenade:

- 1 cup pitted Kalamata olives
- 2 cloves garlic
- 2 tablespoons capers
- 2 tablespoons fresh parsley, chopped
- 2 tablespoons extra virgin olive oil
- 1 tablespoon lemon juice
- Freshly ground black pepper, to taste

For Serving:

- Pita bread, warmed
- Fresh parsley, chopped, for garnish (optional)
- Extra virgin olive oil, for drizzling

Instructions:

1. To make the hummus, combine the chickpeas, minced garlic, tahini, lemon juice, olive oil, ground cumin, and a pinch of salt in a food processor. Blend until smooth, adding water as needed to achieve your desired consistency. Taste and adjust the seasoning with more salt if needed. Transfer the hummus to a serving bowl and set aside.
2. To make the olive tapenade, combine the pitted Kalamata olives, garlic cloves, capers, chopped parsley, extra virgin olive oil, lemon juice, and freshly ground black pepper in a food processor. Pulse until the mixture is finely chopped and well combined, but still slightly chunky. Transfer the tapenade to a serving bowl and set aside.
3. Warm the pita bread in a skillet or oven until heated through.
4. To serve, spread a generous amount of hummus on each warmed pita bread round. Top with a spoonful of olive tapenade.
5. Garnish with chopped fresh parsley, if desired, and drizzle with a little extra virgin olive oil.
6. Serve the pita bread with hummus and olive tapenade immediately, while the bread is warm and the flavors are fresh.

This pita bread with hummus and olive tapenade is perfect for serving as an appetizer at parties, gatherings, or as a tasty snack any time of day. Enjoy the combination of creamy hummus and briny olive tapenade with the soft, warm pita bread for a delicious Mediterranean treat!

Yemista (Stuffed Vegetables)

Ingredients:

- 4 large tomatoes
- 4 bell peppers (any color)
- 2 zucchini
- 1 eggplant
- 1 cup long-grain rice (such as jasmine or basmati)
- 1 onion, finely chopped
- 2 cloves garlic, minced
- 1/4 cup extra virgin olive oil, plus extra for drizzling
- 1/4 cup chopped fresh parsley
- 1/4 cup chopped fresh mint
- 1/4 cup chopped fresh dill
- 1/2 cup tomato sauce
- Salt and pepper, to taste
- 1 cup vegetable or chicken broth, plus extra as needed
- Lemon wedges, for serving
- Greek yogurt, for serving (optional)

Instructions:

1. Preheat your oven to 375°F (190°C).
2. Cut the tops off the tomatoes and bell peppers and scoop out the seeds and membranes, creating hollow shells. Cut the zucchini and eggplant in half lengthwise and scoop out the flesh, leaving a hollow cavity. Reserve the scooped-out flesh from the tomatoes, zucchini, and eggplant.
3. In a large mixing bowl, combine the rice, chopped onion, minced garlic, chopped fresh parsley, chopped fresh mint, chopped fresh dill, tomato sauce, and olive oil. Season with salt and pepper, to taste, and mix well.
4. Fill each hollowed-out vegetable with the rice mixture, packing it in tightly.
5. Place the stuffed vegetables in a baking dish. If there is any leftover rice mixture, you can add it to the baking dish around the vegetables.
6. Pour the vegetable or chicken broth into the bottom of the baking dish, filling it about halfway up the sides of the vegetables.
7. Drizzle a little extra olive oil over the stuffed vegetables.

8. Cover the baking dish with aluminum foil and bake in the preheated oven for about 1 hour, or until the vegetables are tender and the rice is cooked through. If the rice starts to dry out during baking, add more broth as needed.
9. Once the yemista are done, remove them from the oven and let them cool for a few minutes before serving.
10. Serve the yemista hot, garnished with fresh herbs and lemon wedges on the side. You can also serve them with a dollop of Greek yogurt, if desired.

Yemista is a flavorful and satisfying dish that's perfect for a vegetarian main course or as a side dish to accompany grilled meats. Enjoy this taste of Greek cuisine!

Greek Yogurt with Honey and Nuts

Ingredients:

- 1 cup Greek yogurt
- 2 tablespoons honey (or more, to taste)
- 1/4 cup mixed nuts (such as almonds, walnuts, or pistachios), chopped
- Fresh fruit, for serving (optional)

Instructions:

1. Spoon the Greek yogurt into a serving bowl or individual serving dishes.
2. Drizzle the honey evenly over the Greek yogurt.
3. Sprinkle the chopped nuts on top of the honey.
4. If desired, serve the Greek yogurt with fresh fruit on the side or on top.
5. Enjoy your Greek yogurt with honey and nuts immediately as a dessert or snack.

This dish is not only delicious but also nutritious, as Greek yogurt is high in protein and probiotics, while honey adds natural sweetness and the nuts provide crunch and healthy fats. It's a versatile dish that can be enjoyed any time of day, whether as a quick breakfast, a satisfying snack, or a light dessert after a meal. Enjoy!

Grilled Halloumi Cheese with Watermelon

Ingredients:

- 1 block of halloumi cheese, sliced into 1/4-inch thick slices
- 2 cups cubed watermelon
- Fresh mint leaves, chopped, for garnish
- Extra virgin olive oil, for drizzling
- Balsamic glaze, for drizzling (optional)
- Lemon wedges, for serving (optional)

Instructions:

1. Preheat your grill or grill pan to medium-high heat.
2. While the grill is heating up, prepare the halloumi cheese and watermelon. Pat the halloumi slices dry with paper towels to remove any excess moisture.
3. Once the grill is hot, place the halloumi slices directly onto the grill grates or into the grill pan. Cook for 2-3 minutes on each side, or until grill marks form and the cheese is lightly browned and slightly softened.
4. While the halloumi is grilling, prepare the watermelon by cutting it into bite-sized cubes.
5. Once the halloumi is grilled to your liking, remove it from the grill and transfer it to a serving platter.
6. Arrange the cubed watermelon around the grilled halloumi on the platter.
7. Drizzle the grilled halloumi and watermelon with extra virgin olive oil.
8. If desired, drizzle the dish with balsamic glaze for added sweetness and flavor.
9. Garnish with chopped fresh mint leaves for a pop of color and freshness.
10. Serve the grilled halloumi cheese with watermelon immediately, while the cheese is warm and the watermelon is cool and refreshing.
11. Optionally, serve with lemon wedges on the side for squeezing over the cheese and watermelon.

This grilled halloumi cheese with watermelon is perfect for serving as a light appetizer, a refreshing side dish, or even as a unique main course for a summer meal. Enjoy the contrast of flavors and textures in this simple yet delicious dish!

Koulouri (Greek Sesame Bread Rings)

Ingredients:

- 4 cups all-purpose flour
- 1 tablespoon active dry yeast
- 1 teaspoon sugar
- 1 1/4 cups warm water
- 1/4 cup olive oil
- 1 teaspoon salt
- 1 cup sesame seeds
- Additional olive oil, for brushing

Instructions:

1. In a small bowl, combine the warm water, sugar, and active dry yeast. Stir gently and let it sit for about 5-10 minutes, or until foamy.
2. In a large mixing bowl, combine the flour and salt. Make a well in the center and pour in the yeast mixture and olive oil.
3. Mix everything together until a dough forms. Knead the dough on a lightly floured surface for about 5-7 minutes, or until it is smooth and elastic.
4. Place the dough in a lightly oiled bowl, cover with a clean kitchen towel or plastic wrap, and let it rise in a warm place for about 1-2 hours, or until it has doubled in size.
5. Preheat your oven to 375°F (190°C). Line a baking sheet with parchment paper.
6. Punch down the risen dough and divide it into 10 equal portions. Roll each portion into a long rope, about 12 inches in length.
7. Join the ends of each rope together to form a ring shape. Press the ends together firmly to seal.
8. Place the sesame seeds on a plate. Brush each bread ring with olive oil, then dip it into the sesame seeds, coating it generously on all sides.
9. Place the sesame-coated bread rings on the prepared baking sheet, leaving some space between them.
10. Bake in the preheated oven for 20-25 minutes, or until the bread rings are golden brown and sound hollow when tapped on the bottom.
11. Remove the koulouri from the oven and transfer them to a wire rack to cool slightly before serving.

Enjoy these delicious Greek sesame bread rings warm or at room temperature. They are perfect for breakfast, as a snack, or served alongside soups and salads.

Galaktoboureko (Custard Pie)

Ingredients:

For the Custard Filling:

- 4 cups whole milk
- 1 cup granulated sugar
- 1 cup semolina flour
- 4 large eggs
- 1 teaspoon vanilla extract
- Zest of 1 lemon

For the Phyllo Pastry:

- 1 package (16 ounces) phyllo dough, thawed according to package instructions
- 1 cup unsalted butter, melted

For the Syrup:

- 2 cups water
- 2 cups granulated sugar
- Juice of 1 lemon
- 1 cinnamon stick
- 2-3 whole cloves

Instructions:

1. Preheat your oven to 350°F (175°C). Grease a 9x13-inch baking dish with butter or cooking spray.
2. To make the custard filling, heat the milk in a saucepan over medium heat until it begins to simmer. In a separate bowl, whisk together the sugar, semolina flour, eggs, vanilla extract, and lemon zest until smooth. Slowly pour the hot milk into the semolina mixture, whisking constantly.

3. Return the mixture to the saucepan and cook over medium heat, stirring constantly, until it thickens to a pudding-like consistency, about 5-7 minutes. Remove from heat and let the custard cool slightly.
4. To assemble the galaktoboureko, layer half of the phyllo dough sheets in the bottom of the prepared baking dish, brushing each sheet generously with melted butter. Pour the custard filling over the phyllo dough and spread it out evenly.
5. Layer the remaining phyllo dough sheets on top of the custard filling, again brushing each sheet generously with melted butter.
6. Using a sharp knife, carefully score the top layer of phyllo dough into diamond-shaped pieces.
7. Bake in the preheated oven for 45-50 minutes, or until the top is golden brown and crispy.
8. While the galaktoboureko is baking, prepare the syrup. In a saucepan, combine the water, sugar, lemon juice, cinnamon stick, and cloves. Bring to a boil, then reduce the heat to low and simmer for 5-7 minutes, or until the syrup thickens slightly.
9. Once the galaktoboureko is done baking, remove it from the oven and immediately pour the hot syrup evenly over the top, allowing it to seep into the cuts in the phyllo dough.
10. Let the galaktoboureko cool completely in the baking dish before slicing and serving.

Enjoy this delicious Greek custard pie with its crispy layers of phyllo pastry and creamy semolina filling, soaked in a sweet syrup. It's a perfect dessert for special occasions or anytime you're craving a taste of Greece!

Gemista (Stuffed Bell Peppers)

Ingredients:

- 6 large bell peppers (any color)
- 1 cup long-grain rice (such as jasmine or basmati)
- 1 onion, finely chopped
- 2 cloves garlic, minced
- 2 tomatoes, diced
- 1/4 cup tomato sauce
- 1/4 cup chopped fresh parsley
- 1/4 cup chopped fresh mint
- 1/4 cup chopped fresh dill
- 1/4 cup pine nuts (optional)
- 1/4 cup raisins (optional)
- 1/4 cup extra virgin olive oil
- Salt and pepper, to taste
- Water or vegetable broth, as needed

Instructions:

1. Preheat your oven to 375°F (190°C).
2. Cut the tops off the bell peppers and remove the seeds and membranes from the inside, creating hollow shells. Reserve the tops of the bell peppers.
3. In a large mixing bowl, combine the rice, chopped onion, minced garlic, diced tomatoes, tomato sauce, chopped fresh parsley, chopped fresh mint, chopped fresh dill, pine nuts (if using), raisins (if using), and extra virgin olive oil. Season with salt and pepper to taste. Mix well to combine.
4. Stuff each bell pepper with the rice mixture, filling them to the top. Place the reserved tops of the bell peppers back on, securing them in place.
5. Arrange the stuffed bell peppers in a baking dish, standing upright.
6. Pour water or vegetable broth into the bottom of the baking dish, filling it about halfway up the sides of the peppers.
7. Cover the baking dish with aluminum foil and bake in the preheated oven for about 45-50 minutes, or until the peppers are tender and the rice is cooked through. If the rice starts to dry out during baking, add more water or broth as needed.

8. Once the stuffed bell peppers are done, remove them from the oven and let them cool slightly before serving.

Serve the gemista hot or at room temperature, garnished with additional fresh herbs if desired. They make a delicious and satisfying vegetarian main course or side dish, perfect for any occasion. Enjoy!

Greek Fava Bean Dip

Ingredients:

- 1 cup dried yellow split peas
- 4 cups water
- 1 onion, finely chopped
- 2 cloves garlic, minced
- 1/4 cup extra virgin olive oil, plus extra for drizzling
- 1 bay leaf
- Salt and pepper, to taste
- Juice of 1 lemon
- Chopped fresh parsley, for garnish
- Optional toppings: sliced red onion, capers, chopped tomatoes

Instructions:

1. Rinse the dried yellow split peas under cold water and drain them well.
2. In a large pot, combine the rinsed split peas, water, chopped onion, minced garlic, olive oil, and bay leaf. Bring the mixture to a boil over medium-high heat.
3. Reduce the heat to low and simmer, uncovered, for about 45-60 minutes, or until the split peas are very tender and beginning to fall apart. Stir occasionally and skim off any foam that rises to the surface.
4. Once the split peas are cooked, remove the bay leaf from the pot and discard it.
5. Use an immersion blender or transfer the mixture to a food processor or blender, and blend until smooth and creamy. If the mixture is too thick, you can add a little water or broth to reach your desired consistency.
6. Season the fava dip with salt, pepper, and lemon juice to taste. Adjust the seasoning as needed.
7. Transfer the fava dip to a serving bowl and drizzle with extra virgin olive oil. Garnish with chopped fresh parsley.
8. Serve the Greek fava bean dip warm or at room temperature, accompanied by sliced bread, pita wedges, or vegetable sticks for dipping. You can also top it with sliced red onion, capers, chopped tomatoes, or other toppings of your choice.

Enjoy this creamy and flavorful Greek fava bean dip as part of a mezze platter or as a tasty appetizer at your next gathering!

Kolokythokeftedes (Zucchini Fritters)

Ingredients:

- 2 medium zucchini, grated
- 1 teaspoon salt
- 1/2 cup crumbled feta cheese
- 1/4 cup chopped fresh dill
- 1/4 cup chopped fresh mint
- 1/4 cup chopped fresh parsley
- 2 green onions, finely chopped
- 2 cloves garlic, minced
- 1/2 cup all-purpose flour
- 2 large eggs, beaten
- Salt and pepper, to taste
- Olive oil, for frying
- Greek yogurt or tzatziki sauce, for serving (optional)

Instructions:

1. Place the grated zucchini in a colander set over a bowl and sprinkle with 1 teaspoon of salt. Let it sit for about 10-15 minutes to allow the salt to draw out excess moisture from the zucchini.
2. After 10-15 minutes, squeeze the grated zucchini with your hands to remove as much moisture as possible. Transfer the squeezed zucchini to a clean kitchen towel and pat it dry.
3. In a large mixing bowl, combine the grated zucchini, crumbled feta cheese, chopped fresh dill, chopped fresh mint, chopped fresh parsley, green onions, minced garlic, flour, beaten eggs, and salt and pepper to taste. Mix until well combined.
4. Heat a thin layer of olive oil in a large skillet over medium heat.
5. Scoop about 2 tablespoons of the zucchini mixture and form it into a patty with your hands. Repeat with the remaining mixture.
6. Carefully place the zucchini fritters in the hot oil, making sure not to overcrowd the skillet. Flatten them slightly with a spatula.
7. Cook the fritters for 3-4 minutes on each side, or until golden brown and crispy. Use a spatula to flip them halfway through cooking.

8. Once the fritters are cooked through and crispy on both sides, remove them from the skillet and transfer them to a plate lined with paper towels to drain any excess oil.
9. Serve the kolokythokeftedes hot, garnished with additional chopped herbs if desired. Serve with Greek yogurt or tzatziki sauce on the side for dipping, if desired.

Enjoy these crispy and flavorful Greek zucchini fritters as a delicious appetizer or side dish!

Keftethes (Greek Meatballs)

Ingredients:

- 1 lb ground beef or lamb (or a mixture of both)
- 1 small onion, grated or finely chopped
- 2 cloves garlic, minced
- 1/4 cup breadcrumbs
- 1/4 cup grated Parmesan cheese
- 1/4 cup chopped fresh parsley
- 1 teaspoon dried oregano
- 1/2 teaspoon dried mint
- 1/4 teaspoon ground cinnamon
- 1/4 teaspoon ground nutmeg
- Salt and pepper, to taste
- 1 egg, beaten
- All-purpose flour, for coating
- Olive oil, for frying

Instructions:

1. In a large mixing bowl, combine the ground meat, grated onion, minced garlic, breadcrumbs, grated Parmesan cheese, chopped fresh parsley, dried oregano, dried mint, ground cinnamon, ground nutmeg, salt, pepper, and beaten egg. Mix until well combined.
2. Shape the mixture into small meatballs, about 1 inch in diameter. You can wet your hands with water to prevent sticking.
3. Roll the meatballs in flour to coat them evenly, shaking off any excess flour.
4. Heat a thin layer of olive oil in a large skillet over medium heat.
5. Once the oil is hot, add the meatballs to the skillet in batches, making sure not to overcrowd the pan. Cook the meatballs for 3-4 minutes on each side, or until golden brown and cooked through.
6. Use a slotted spoon to transfer the cooked meatballs to a plate lined with paper towels to drain any excess oil.
7. Repeat the process with the remaining meatballs, adding more oil to the skillet as needed.
8. Serve the keftethes hot, garnished with additional chopped parsley if desired. Serve with tzatziki sauce or marinara sauce on the side for dipping.

Enjoy these flavorful Greek meatballs as a delicious appetizer or main course!

Garides Saganaki (Shrimp in Tomato Sauce with Feta)

Ingredients:

- 1 lb large shrimp, peeled and deveined
- 2 tablespoons olive oil
- 1 small onion, finely chopped
- 2 cloves garlic, minced
- 1 red bell pepper, diced
- 1 can (14 oz) diced tomatoes
- 1/4 cup dry white wine (optional)
- 1 teaspoon dried oregano
- 1/2 teaspoon dried basil
- Salt and pepper, to taste
- 1/2 cup crumbled feta cheese
- Chopped fresh parsley, for garnish
- Crusty bread, for serving

Instructions:

1. Heat the olive oil in a large skillet over medium heat. Add the chopped onion and diced bell pepper, and sauté until softened, about 5 minutes.
2. Add the minced garlic to the skillet and sauté for an additional 1-2 minutes, until fragrant.
3. Stir in the diced tomatoes (with their juices), white wine (if using), dried oregano, and dried basil. Season with salt and pepper to taste.
4. Bring the mixture to a simmer and let it cook for about 10 minutes, allowing the flavors to meld together and the sauce to thicken slightly.
5. Add the peeled and deveined shrimp to the skillet, stirring to coat them in the tomato sauce. Cook for 3-4 minutes, or until the shrimp are pink and opaque.
6. Sprinkle the crumbled feta cheese evenly over the top of the shrimp and tomato sauce mixture.
7. Cover the skillet with a lid and let it cook for an additional 1-2 minutes, or until the feta cheese is softened and slightly melted.
8. Remove the skillet from the heat and garnish the garides saganaki with chopped fresh parsley.

9. Serve the shrimp and tomato sauce mixture hot, directly from the skillet, with crusty bread for dipping.

Enjoy this flavorful Greek dish of garides saganaki as a delicious appetizer or main course!

Greek Lamb Chops with Tzatziki

Ingredients:

For the Lamb Chops:

- 8 lamb loin chops
- 2 tablespoons olive oil
- 2 cloves garlic, minced
- 1 teaspoon dried oregano
- 1 teaspoon dried thyme
- Salt and pepper, to taste
- Lemon wedges, for serving

For the Tzatziki:

- 1 cup Greek yogurt
- 1/2 cucumber, grated and squeezed to remove excess moisture
- 1 clove garlic, minced
- 1 tablespoon chopped fresh dill
- 1 tablespoon chopped fresh mint
- 1 tablespoon extra virgin olive oil
- 1 tablespoon lemon juice
- Salt and pepper, to taste

Instructions:

1. In a mixing bowl, combine the olive oil, minced garlic, dried oregano, dried thyme, salt, and pepper. Rub this mixture all over the lamb chops, coating them evenly. Allow the lamb chops to marinate for at least 30 minutes, or overnight in the refrigerator for deeper flavor.
2. While the lamb chops are marinating, prepare the tzatziki sauce. In a separate mixing bowl, combine the Greek yogurt, grated cucumber, minced garlic, chopped fresh dill, chopped fresh mint, extra virgin olive oil, lemon juice, salt, and pepper.

Mix until well combined. Taste and adjust the seasoning as needed. Refrigerate the tzatziki until ready to serve.
3. Preheat your grill or grill pan to medium-high heat. Once hot, grill the lamb chops for 3-4 minutes on each side, or until cooked to your desired doneness. Cooking time will vary depending on the thickness of the chops and your preferred level of doneness.
4. Remove the lamb chops from the grill and let them rest for a few minutes before serving.
5. Serve the grilled lamb chops hot, garnished with lemon wedges and accompanied by the tzatziki sauce on the side.
6. Enjoy your Greek lamb chops with tzatziki alongside your favorite sides, such as Greek salad, roasted vegetables, or pita bread.

This dish is perfect for a Mediterranean-inspired dinner or for entertaining guests. The juicy and flavorful lamb chops paired with the creamy and tangy tzatziki sauce make for a winning combination that's sure to impress!

Revithia (Greek Chickpea Soup)

Ingredients:

- 2 cups dried chickpeas, soaked overnight (or 2 cans, drained and rinsed)
- 1 large onion, finely chopped
- 3 cloves garlic, minced
- 1/4 cup olive oil
- 1 bay leaf
- 1 teaspoon dried oregano
- 1 teaspoon dried thyme
- 6 cups vegetable or chicken broth
- Salt and pepper, to taste
- Chopped fresh parsley, for garnish
- Lemon wedges, for serving

Instructions:

1. If using dried chickpeas, soak them in water overnight. Drain and rinse the soaked chickpeas before using. If using canned chickpeas, drain and rinse them well.
2. In a large pot, heat the olive oil over medium heat. Add the chopped onion and cook until softened, about 5 minutes.
3. Add the minced garlic to the pot and cook for an additional 1-2 minutes, until fragrant.
4. Stir in the soaked chickpeas (or canned chickpeas) and bay leaf. Cook for another 2-3 minutes, allowing the chickpeas to absorb the flavors.
5. Add the dried oregano, dried thyme, and vegetable or chicken broth to the pot. Season with salt and pepper to taste.
6. Bring the soup to a boil, then reduce the heat to low and simmer, partially covered, for about 1 to 1 1/2 hours, or until the chickpeas are tender. If using canned chickpeas, you may need less cooking time.
7. Once the chickpeas are tender, remove the bay leaf from the pot and discard it.
8. Use an immersion blender to partially blend the soup, leaving some chickpeas whole for texture. Alternatively, you can transfer a portion of the soup to a blender and blend until smooth, then return it to the pot.
9. Taste the soup and adjust the seasoning as needed with salt and pepper.

10. Serve the revithia hot, garnished with chopped fresh parsley and lemon wedges on the side for squeezing over the soup.

Enjoy this comforting and nutritious Greek chickpea soup as a satisfying meal on its own or as a starter to a Greek-inspired feast!

Melitzanosalata (Greek Eggplant Dip)

Ingredients:

- 2 large eggplants
- 2 cloves garlic, minced
- 2 tablespoons extra virgin olive oil, plus extra for drizzling
- Juice of 1 lemon
- 2 tablespoons chopped fresh parsley
- Salt and pepper, to taste
- Optional: chopped fresh mint, chopped fresh dill, red pepper flakes

Instructions:

1. Preheat your oven to 400°F (200°C). Line a baking sheet with parchment paper.
2. Use a fork to pierce the eggplants several times. Place them on the prepared baking sheet and roast in the preheated oven for 45-60 minutes, or until the eggplants are very tender and collapsed.
3. Remove the eggplants from the oven and let them cool slightly. Once cool enough to handle, slice them open and scoop out the flesh into a bowl, discarding the skins.
4. Use a fork or potato masher to mash the roasted eggplant until smooth.
5. Add the minced garlic, olive oil, lemon juice, chopped fresh parsley, salt, and pepper to the mashed eggplant. Mix well to combine.
6. Taste the melitzanosalata and adjust the seasoning as needed. If desired, you can also add chopped fresh mint, chopped fresh dill, or a pinch of red pepper flakes for extra flavor.
7. Transfer the melitzanosalata to a serving bowl and drizzle with a little extra virgin olive oil.
8. Serve the Greek eggplant dip at room temperature, accompanied by toasted bread, pita chips, or fresh vegetables for dipping.

Enjoy this creamy and flavorful melitzanosalata as a delicious appetizer or snack with a Mediterranean twist!

Pita Bread with Greek Salad Filling

Ingredients:

For the Greek Salad Filling:

- 2 large tomatoes, diced
- 1 cucumber, diced
- 1/2 red onion, thinly sliced
- 1/2 cup Kalamata olives, pitted and halved
- 1/2 cup crumbled feta cheese
- 2 tablespoons chopped fresh parsley
- 2 tablespoons extra virgin olive oil
- 1 tablespoon red wine vinegar
- Salt and pepper, to taste

For Serving:

- Pita bread, warmed
- Optional additional toppings: sliced bell peppers, sliced pepperoncini, chopped fresh mint, sliced radishes

Instructions:

1. In a large mixing bowl, combine the diced tomatoes, diced cucumber, thinly sliced red onion, halved Kalamata olives, crumbled feta cheese, and chopped fresh parsley.
2. Drizzle the extra virgin olive oil and red wine vinegar over the salad mixture. Season with salt and pepper to taste.
3. Gently toss the salad until all the ingredients are evenly coated with the dressing.
4. Warm the pita bread in the oven, microwave, or on a skillet until soft and pliable.
5. To assemble the pita sandwiches, open each pita bread to create a pocket. Spoon the Greek salad filling into the pocket, making sure to distribute the ingredients evenly.

6. If desired, add additional toppings such as sliced bell peppers, sliced pepperoncini, chopped fresh mint, or sliced radishes.
7. Serve the filled pita sandwiches immediately, while the pita bread is still warm and the salad ingredients are fresh.

Enjoy these delicious pita bread sandwiches filled with a refreshing Greek salad for a light and flavorful meal! They're perfect for lunch, dinner, or as a portable snack on the go.

Psarosoupa (Greek Fish Soup)

Ingredients:

- 1 lb mixed fish fillets (such as cod, haddock, or sea bass), cut into bite-sized pieces
- 1 onion, finely chopped
- 2 cloves garlic, minced
- 2 carrots, diced
- 2 celery stalks, diced
- 1 potato, diced
- 1 can (14 oz) diced tomatoes
- 6 cups fish or vegetable broth
- 1/4 cup chopped fresh parsley
- 1/4 cup chopped fresh dill
- 2 bay leaves
- Salt and pepper, to taste
- Lemon wedges, for serving
- Crusty bread, for serving

Instructions:

1. In a large pot, heat a drizzle of olive oil over medium heat. Add the chopped onion and minced garlic, and cook until softened and fragrant, about 5 minutes.
2. Add the diced carrots, diced celery, and diced potato to the pot. Cook for another 5 minutes, stirring occasionally.
3. Pour in the diced tomatoes (with their juices) and fish or vegetable broth. Add the bay leaves, chopped fresh parsley, and chopped fresh dill to the pot. Season with salt and pepper to taste.
4. Bring the soup to a boil, then reduce the heat to low and let it simmer, uncovered, for about 15-20 minutes, or until the vegetables are tender.
5. Once the vegetables are tender, add the bite-sized pieces of fish to the pot. Simmer gently for another 5-7 minutes, or until the fish is cooked through and flakes easily with a fork.
6. Taste the soup and adjust the seasoning as needed with salt and pepper.
7. Remove the bay leaves from the pot and discard them.

8. Ladle the psarosoupa into bowls and serve hot, garnished with additional chopped fresh parsley and a squeeze of lemon juice. Serve with crusty bread on the side for dipping.

Enjoy this delicious and comforting Greek fish soup as a nourishing meal any time of the year!

Greek Orzo Salad

Ingredients:

For the Salad:

- 1 cup orzo pasta
- 1 cucumber, diced
- 1 cup cherry tomatoes, halved
- 1/2 red onion, finely chopped
- 1/2 cup Kalamata olives, pitted and halved
- 1/2 cup crumbled feta cheese
- 1/4 cup chopped fresh parsley
- 1/4 cup chopped fresh dill (optional)
- Salt and pepper, to taste

For the Dressing:

- 1/4 cup extra virgin olive oil
- 2 tablespoons red wine vinegar
- 1 tablespoon lemon juice
- 1 teaspoon dried oregano
- 1 clove garlic, minced
- Salt and pepper, to taste

Instructions:

1. Cook the orzo pasta according to the package instructions until al dente. Drain the cooked pasta and rinse it under cold water to stop the cooking process. Set aside to cool.
2. In a large mixing bowl, combine the cooled orzo pasta, diced cucumber, halved cherry tomatoes, finely chopped red onion, halved Kalamata olives, crumbled feta cheese, chopped fresh parsley, and chopped fresh dill (if using). Toss gently to combine.

3. In a small bowl, whisk together the extra virgin olive oil, red wine vinegar, lemon juice, dried oregano, minced garlic, salt, and pepper to make the dressing.
4. Pour the dressing over the orzo salad and toss until everything is evenly coated.
5. Taste the salad and adjust the seasoning with salt and pepper, if needed.
6. Cover the salad and refrigerate for at least 30 minutes to allow the flavors to meld together.
7. Before serving, give the salad a final toss and garnish with additional chopped fresh parsley or dill, if desired.
8. Serve the Greek orzo salad chilled or at room temperature as a refreshing side dish or light meal.

Enjoy this vibrant and flavorful Greek orzo salad as a delicious addition to your summer picnics, potlucks, or backyard barbecues!

Tyropita (Feta Cheese Pie)

Ingredients:

- 1 package (16 oz) phyllo dough, thawed according to package instructions
- 1/2 cup unsalted butter, melted
- 1 lb feta cheese, crumbled
- 3 large eggs, beaten
- 1/4 cup chopped fresh parsley
- 1/4 cup chopped fresh dill
- Freshly ground black pepper, to taste

Instructions:

1. Preheat your oven to 350°F (175°C). Lightly grease a 9x13-inch baking dish.
2. In a mixing bowl, combine the crumbled feta cheese, beaten eggs, chopped fresh parsley, chopped fresh dill, and black pepper. Mix well until all the ingredients are evenly incorporated.
3. Unroll the phyllo dough and place it on a clean, dry surface. Cover the phyllo dough with a damp kitchen towel to prevent it from drying out while you work.
4. Place one sheet of phyllo dough in the bottom of the prepared baking dish, allowing the excess to hang over the edges. Brush the phyllo sheet lightly with melted butter.
5. Repeat layering phyllo sheets and brushing each layer with melted butter until you have used about half of the phyllo dough.
6. Spread the feta cheese mixture evenly over the layered phyllo dough in the baking dish.
7. Continue layering the remaining phyllo sheets on top of the feta cheese mixture, brushing each sheet with melted butter as before. Fold any excess phyllo dough over the top to form a crust around the edges.
8. Using a sharp knife, carefully score the top layer of phyllo dough into squares or triangles, being careful not to cut all the way through to the bottom.
9. Bake the tyropita in the preheated oven for 45-50 minutes, or until the phyllo dough is golden brown and crispy.
10. Remove the tyropita from the oven and let it cool slightly before slicing and serving.

Enjoy this delicious and savory feta cheese pie warm or at room temperature as a delightful appetizer, side dish, or even a light main course in a Greek-inspired meal!

Greek Spinach and Feta Stuffed Chicken

Ingredients:

- 4 boneless, skinless chicken breasts
- 2 cups fresh spinach leaves, chopped
- 1/2 cup crumbled feta cheese
- 2 cloves garlic, minced
- 1 tablespoon chopped fresh dill
- 1 tablespoon chopped fresh parsley
- 1 tablespoon lemon juice
- Salt and pepper, to taste
- Olive oil, for cooking
- Toothpicks or kitchen twine, for securing the chicken

Instructions:

1. Preheat your oven to 375°F (190°C). Lightly grease a baking dish large enough to fit the chicken breasts in a single layer.
2. In a mixing bowl, combine the chopped spinach, crumbled feta cheese, minced garlic, chopped fresh dill, chopped fresh parsley, lemon juice, salt, and pepper. Mix well to combine.
3. Use a sharp knife to carefully butterfly each chicken breast, cutting horizontally through the thickest part of the breast, but not all the way through, to create a pocket.
4. Stuff each chicken breast with a portion of the spinach and feta filling, pressing it firmly into the pocket. Secure the openings with toothpicks or kitchen twine to prevent the filling from spilling out during cooking.
5. Heat a drizzle of olive oil in a large skillet over medium-high heat. Once hot, add the stuffed chicken breasts to the skillet and cook for 2-3 minutes on each side, or until lightly browned.
6. Transfer the browned chicken breasts to the prepared baking dish. If any filling has spilled out, you can spoon it over the top of the chicken.
7. Bake the stuffed chicken breasts in the preheated oven for 20-25 minutes, or until the chicken is cooked through and no longer pink in the center.
8. Remove the toothpicks or kitchen twine from the chicken before serving.

9. Serve the Greek spinach and feta stuffed chicken hot, garnished with additional chopped fresh parsley and lemon wedges on the side for squeezing over the chicken.

Enjoy this delicious and elegant dish as a main course for a special dinner or any day of the week when you're craving a taste of Greece!

Kalamata Olive Tapenade

Ingredients:

- 1 cup pitted Kalamata olives
- 2 tablespoons capers, drained
- 2 cloves garlic, minced
- 2 tablespoons fresh lemon juice
- 2 tablespoons extra virgin olive oil
- 1 tablespoon chopped fresh parsley
- 1 teaspoon chopped fresh thyme (optional)
- Freshly ground black pepper, to taste

Instructions:

1. In a food processor, combine the pitted Kalamata olives, capers, minced garlic, fresh lemon juice, and extra virgin olive oil.
2. Pulse the mixture several times until it reaches your desired consistency. For a chunky tapenade, pulse less; for a smoother tapenade, pulse more.
3. Add the chopped fresh parsley and chopped fresh thyme (if using) to the food processor. Season with freshly ground black pepper to taste.
4. Pulse the mixture a few more times to incorporate the herbs and seasonings evenly.
5. Taste the tapenade and adjust the seasoning as needed. You can add more lemon juice, olive oil, or herbs according to your preferences.
6. Transfer the Kalamata olive tapenade to a serving bowl or airtight container.
7. Serve the tapenade immediately as a spread or condiment, or refrigerate it for later use. It will keep well in the refrigerator for up to one week.
8. Enjoy the Kalamata olive tapenade spread on toasted bread, crackers, or sandwiches, or use it to add flavor to pasta dishes, grilled meats, or roasted vegetables.

This flavorful and versatile condiment is a must-have for any Mediterranean-inspired meal or appetizer spread!

Octopus Salad

Ingredients:

- 1 lb octopus, cleaned and tentacles separated
- 1 lemon, halved
- 1/4 cup extra virgin olive oil
- 2 cloves garlic, minced
- 1 teaspoon dried oregano
- Salt and pepper, to taste
- 1 cucumber, thinly sliced
- 1 bell pepper, thinly sliced
- 1 red onion, thinly sliced
- 1/4 cup Kalamata olives, pitted and halved
- 2 tablespoons chopped fresh parsley
- Lemon wedges, for serving

Instructions:

1. Bring a large pot of salted water to a boil. Add the cleaned octopus and one lemon half to the pot. Reduce the heat to low and simmer gently for about 30-40 minutes, or until the octopus is tender. (You can test for doneness by inserting a fork into the thickest part of the octopus; it should slide in easily.)
2. Remove the octopus from the pot and let it cool slightly. Once cool enough to handle, cut the octopus into bite-sized pieces, discarding any tough parts.
3. In a small bowl, whisk together the extra virgin olive oil, minced garlic, dried oregano, salt, and pepper to make the dressing.
4. In a large mixing bowl, combine the sliced cucumber, bell pepper, red onion, and halved Kalamata olives.
5. Add the chopped octopus to the bowl with the vegetables.
6. Pour the dressing over the octopus and vegetable mixture, tossing gently to coat everything evenly.
7. Sprinkle the chopped fresh parsley over the salad and toss again to incorporate.
8. Taste the salad and adjust the seasoning with salt and pepper, if needed.
9. Transfer the octopus salad to a serving platter or individual plates.
10. Serve the salad immediately, garnished with lemon wedges on the side for squeezing over the salad.

Enjoy this delicious octopus salad as a refreshing appetizer or light meal, perfect for summer gatherings or as part of a Mediterranean-inspired feast!

Greek Spinach Rice (Spanakorizo)

Ingredients:

- 2 tablespoons olive oil
- 1 onion, finely chopped
- 2 cloves garlic, minced
- 1 cup long-grain white rice
- 2 cups vegetable broth or water
- 1 lb fresh spinach leaves, washed and chopped
- 1/4 cup chopped fresh dill
- 1/4 cup chopped fresh parsley
- Juice of 1 lemon
- Salt and pepper, to taste
- Lemon wedges, for serving (optional)

Instructions:

1. In a large pot or Dutch oven, heat the olive oil over medium heat. Add the chopped onion and cook until softened, about 5 minutes.
2. Add the minced garlic to the pot and cook for another minute, until fragrant.
3. Stir in the white rice and cook for 1-2 minutes, stirring frequently, until the rice is coated in the olive oil and begins to toast slightly.
4. Pour in the vegetable broth or water and bring the mixture to a simmer. Reduce the heat to low, cover, and let the rice cook for 15 minutes.
5. After 15 minutes, add the chopped spinach to the pot, stirring it into the rice mixture. Cover the pot again and cook for an additional 5-7 minutes, or until the spinach is wilted and the rice is tender.
6. Once the rice is cooked and the spinach is wilted, remove the pot from the heat. Stir in the chopped fresh dill, chopped fresh parsley, and lemon juice. Season with salt and pepper to taste.
7. Serve the spanakorizo hot, garnished with lemon wedges if desired.

Enjoy this flavorful and nutritious Greek spinach rice as a side dish or a light vegetarian meal. It pairs well with grilled meats, fish, or tofu, and is delicious served with a dollop of Greek yogurt on the side.

Melomakarona (Greek Honey Cookies)

Ingredients:

- 1 cup olive oil
- 1/2 cup sugar
- 1/4 cup brandy or orange juice
- Zest of 1 orange
- 1/4 cup orange juice
- 1/4 cup water
- 1 teaspoon baking soda
- 1 teaspoon baking powder
- 1/2 teaspoon ground cloves
- 1 teaspoon ground cinnamon
- 1/4 teaspoon salt
- 4 cups all-purpose flour

For the Syrup:

- 1 cup honey
- 1 cup sugar
- 1 cup water
- Zest of 1 orange
- Juice of 1/2 lemon

Topping:

- Chopped walnuts
- Ground cinnamon

Instructions:

1. Preheat your oven to 350°F (175°C).
2. In a mixing bowl, combine the olive oil and sugar. Mix until well combined.
3. Add the brandy (or orange juice), orange zest, orange juice, and water. Mix well.
4. In a separate bowl, sift together the flour, baking soda, baking powder, cloves, cinnamon, and salt.
5. Gradually add the dry ingredients to the wet ingredients, mixing until a soft dough forms.

6. Take portions of the dough and shape them into oval or round cookies, about 1 inch thick.
7. Place the cookies on a baking sheet lined with parchment paper and bake for 20-25 minutes, or until lightly golden brown.
8. While the cookies are baking, prepare the syrup. In a saucepan, combine the honey, sugar, water, orange zest, and lemon juice. Bring to a boil, then reduce the heat and let it simmer for about 5 minutes.
9. Once the cookies are baked, remove them from the oven and immediately dip them in the hot syrup, making sure they are well coated.
10. Place the cookies on a wire rack to cool. Sprinkle with chopped walnuts and ground cinnamon while they're still warm.
11. Let the cookies cool completely before serving. Enjoy your delicious melomakarona!

These cookies are best enjoyed with a cup of Greek coffee or tea, and they make a wonderful treat during the holiday season.

Greek-style Stuffed Mushrooms

Ingredients:

- 12 large mushrooms, stems removed and reserved
- 1 tablespoon olive oil
- 1 small onion, finely chopped
- 2 cloves garlic, minced
- 2 cups fresh spinach, chopped
- 1/2 cup feta cheese, crumbled
- 1/4 cup breadcrumbs
- 2 tablespoons fresh parsley, chopped
- Salt and pepper to taste
- Lemon wedges for serving

Instructions:

1. Preheat your oven to 375°F (190°C). Lightly grease a baking dish with olive oil or cooking spray.
2. Clean the mushrooms and remove the stems. Finely chop the mushroom stems and set them aside.
3. Heat the olive oil in a skillet over medium heat. Add the chopped onion and garlic, and sauté until softened, about 3-4 minutes.
4. Add the chopped mushroom stems to the skillet and cook for another 2-3 minutes.
5. Stir in the chopped spinach and cook until wilted, about 2-3 minutes. Season with salt and pepper to taste.
6. Remove the skillet from the heat and transfer the mixture to a mixing bowl. Let it cool slightly.
7. Once the mixture has cooled, add the crumbled feta cheese, breadcrumbs, and chopped parsley. Mix until well combined.
8. Place the mushroom caps in the prepared baking dish, cavity side up. Spoon the filling mixture into each mushroom cap, pressing down gently to pack the filling.
9. Bake the stuffed mushrooms in the preheated oven for 15-20 minutes, or until the mushrooms are tender and the filling is golden brown.
10. Remove from the oven and let the mushrooms cool for a few minutes before serving.
11. Serve the stuffed mushrooms warm, garnished with fresh parsley and lemon wedges on the side.

These Greek-style stuffed mushrooms are packed with flavor and make a fantastic appetizer for any occasion. Enjoy!

Gigantes Plaki (Baked Giant Beans)

Ingredients:

- 2 cups dried butter beans (gigantes or lima beans), soaked overnight
- 1/4 cup olive oil
- 1 large onion, finely chopped
- 3 cloves garlic, minced
- 1 can (14 oz) crushed tomatoes
- 1 tablespoon tomato paste
- 1 teaspoon sugar
- 1 teaspoon dried oregano
- 1 teaspoon dried thyme
- 1 bay leaf
- Salt and pepper to taste
- 1/4 cup chopped fresh parsley
- 1/4 cup chopped fresh dill
- 1/4 cup crumbled feta cheese (optional)
- Lemon wedges for serving

Instructions:

1. Preheat your oven to 350°F (175°C).
2. Drain the soaked beans and rinse them under cold water. Place them in a large pot, cover with water, and bring to a boil. Reduce the heat and simmer for 30-40 minutes, or until the beans are tender but still hold their shape. Drain and set aside.
3. In a large skillet, heat the olive oil over medium heat. Add the chopped onion and cook until soft and translucent, about 5 minutes.
4. Add the minced garlic to the skillet and cook for another minute, until fragrant.
5. Stir in the crushed tomatoes, tomato paste, sugar, dried oregano, dried thyme, bay leaf, salt, and pepper. Let the sauce simmer for 5-7 minutes, until slightly thickened.
6. Remove the bay leaf from the sauce and stir in the cooked beans, chopped parsley, and chopped dill. Mix until the beans are evenly coated with the sauce.
7. Transfer the bean mixture to a baking dish and spread it out evenly.
8. If using, sprinkle the crumbled feta cheese over the top of the beans.
9. Cover the baking dish with aluminum foil and bake in the preheated oven for 45-50 minutes, or until the beans are tender and the sauce is bubbling.

10. Remove the foil during the last 10 minutes of baking to allow the top to brown slightly.
11. Once done, remove from the oven and let it cool for a few minutes before serving.
12. Serve the Gigantes Plaki warm, garnished with additional chopped parsley and dill, and with lemon wedges on the side.

This dish pairs wonderfully with crusty bread and a Greek salad. Enjoy your flavorful Gigantes Plaki!

Greek-style Roasted Leg of Lamb

Ingredients:

- 1 leg of lamb, bone-in (about 5-6 pounds)
- 6 cloves garlic, minced
- 2 tablespoons fresh rosemary, chopped (or 1 tablespoon dried)
- 2 tablespoons fresh oregano, chopped (or 1 tablespoon dried)
- Zest of 1 lemon
- Juice of 1 lemon
- 1/4 cup olive oil
- Salt and freshly ground black pepper, to taste
- 1 cup chicken or vegetable broth (or water)
- 1/2 cup dry white wine (optional)

Instructions:

1. Preheat your oven to 350°F (175°C).
2. In a small bowl, mix together the minced garlic, chopped rosemary, chopped oregano, lemon zest, lemon juice, and olive oil to make a marinade.
3. Place the leg of lamb in a large roasting pan or baking dish. Use a sharp knife to make several deep slits all over the lamb.
4. Rub the marinade mixture all over the lamb, making sure to get it into the slits you made. Season the lamb generously with salt and pepper.
5. If you have time, cover the lamb and let it marinate in the refrigerator for at least 2 hours, or overnight for maximum flavor.
6. Pour the chicken or vegetable broth (or water) into the bottom of the roasting pan. If using, add the white wine as well.
7. Cover the roasting pan with aluminum foil and roast the lamb in the preheated oven for about 1 hour.
8. After 1 hour, remove the foil and continue roasting for another 1 to 1 1/2 hours, or until the internal temperature of the lamb reaches your desired doneness (about 135°F/57°C for medium-rare or 145°F/63°C for medium).
9. Baste the lamb occasionally with the pan juices to keep it moist and flavorful.
10. Once the lamb is cooked to your liking, remove it from the oven and transfer it to a cutting board. Tent it loosely with foil and let it rest for about 15-20 minutes before carving.
11. Slice the lamb and serve it with your favorite side dishes, such as roasted potatoes, Greek salad, and tzatziki sauce.

12. Enjoy your delicious Greek-style roasted leg of lamb with family and friends!

This dish is sure to impress with its tender, flavorful meat and aromatic Mediterranean herbs.

Lahanodolmades (Cabbage Rolls)

Ingredients:

For the Cabbage Rolls:

- 1 large cabbage head
- 1 cup rice, rinsed
- 1/2 lb ground beef or lamb
- 1 onion, finely chopped
- 2 cloves garlic, minced
- 1/4 cup fresh parsley, chopped
- 1/4 cup fresh dill, chopped
- Salt and pepper to taste
- 1/2 teaspoon ground cinnamon
- 1/4 teaspoon ground nutmeg
- 2 tablespoons olive oil

For the Tomato Sauce:

- 2 tablespoons olive oil
- 1 onion, finely chopped
- 2 cloves garlic, minced
- 1 can (14 oz) crushed tomatoes
- 1 tablespoon tomato paste
- 1/2 cup water or vegetable broth
- Salt and pepper to taste
- 1 tablespoon fresh lemon juice

For Serving:

- Greek yogurt (optional)
- Lemon wedges
- Fresh parsley or dill for garnish

Instructions:

1. Start by preparing the cabbage leaves. Bring a large pot of salted water to a boil. Carefully remove the core from the cabbage head and place it in the boiling

water. Cook for about 5 minutes or until the outer leaves are tender and can be easily peeled off. Remove the cabbage from the pot and let it cool slightly. Once cool, carefully peel off the leaves, trying to keep them intact. Trim any thick veins from the leaves.
2. In a large mixing bowl, combine the rinsed rice, ground meat, chopped onion, minced garlic, chopped parsley, chopped dill, salt, pepper, cinnamon, and nutmeg. Mix until well combined.
3. Place a cabbage leaf on a clean surface and add about 2 tablespoons of the meat and rice mixture near the stem end of the leaf. Fold the sides of the leaf over the filling, then roll it up tightly into a cylinder. Repeat with the remaining cabbage leaves and filling mixture.
4. In a large pot or Dutch oven, heat 2 tablespoons of olive oil over medium heat. Add the chopped onion and garlic and sauté until softened, about 3-4 minutes.
5. Stir in the crushed tomatoes, tomato paste, water or vegetable broth, salt, and pepper. Bring the sauce to a simmer.
6. Carefully place the cabbage rolls seam side down into the pot with the tomato sauce. Arrange them snugly in a single layer.
7. Cover the pot and let the cabbage rolls simmer over low heat for about 45-50 minutes, or until the cabbage is tender and the filling is cooked through. Check occasionally and add more water or broth if the sauce becomes too thick.
8. Once the cabbage rolls are cooked, remove them from the heat and stir in the fresh lemon juice.
9. Serve the cabbage rolls hot, garnished with Greek yogurt, lemon wedges, and fresh parsley or dill.

Enjoy your flavorful and comforting lahanodolmades with a slice of crusty bread or over a bed of fluffy rice!

Kolokithopita (Savory Zucchini Pie)

Ingredients:

For the Filling:

- 3 medium zucchinis, grated
- 1 onion, finely chopped
- 2 cloves garlic, minced
- 1/4 cup fresh parsley, chopped
- 1/4 cup fresh dill, chopped
- 1/2 cup feta cheese, crumbled
- 1/2 cup ricotta cheese (or Greek yogurt)
- 2 eggs
- Salt and pepper to taste
- Olive oil for sautéing

For the Assembly:

- 1/2 pound (about 10 sheets) phyllo pastry, thawed if frozen
- 1/2 cup melted butter or olive oil for brushing

Instructions:

1. Preheat your oven to 350°F (175°C). Lightly grease a baking dish (about 9x13 inches) with olive oil or cooking spray.
2. Start by preparing the filling. Place the grated zucchini in a colander set over a bowl or in the sink. Sprinkle with a little salt and let it sit for about 10-15 minutes to release excess moisture. Afterward, squeeze out any excess liquid from the zucchini using your hands or a clean kitchen towel.
3. Heat a drizzle of olive oil in a skillet over medium heat. Add the chopped onion and garlic and sauté until softened, about 3-4 minutes.
4. Add the grated zucchini to the skillet and cook for another 5-7 minutes, or until it is tender and any remaining moisture has evaporated. Remove from heat and let it cool slightly.
5. In a large mixing bowl, combine the cooked zucchini mixture, chopped parsley, chopped dill, crumbled feta cheese, ricotta cheese (or Greek yogurt), and eggs. Season with salt and pepper to taste. Mix until well combined.

6. Place one sheet of phyllo pastry in the bottom of the prepared baking dish, allowing the edges to hang over the sides. Brush the phyllo sheet lightly with melted butter or olive oil. Repeat with another 4-5 sheets of phyllo, brushing each layer with butter or oil.
7. Spread half of the zucchini mixture evenly over the layered phyllo sheets.
8. Layer another 4-5 sheets of phyllo over the zucchini mixture, brushing each layer with butter or oil.
9. Spread the remaining zucchini mixture over the second layer of phyllo.
10. Finish by layering the remaining phyllo sheets on top, brushing each layer with butter or oil.
11. Fold the overhanging edges of the phyllo sheets over the top of the pie to create a neat border.
12. Brush the top of the pie with any remaining melted butter or oil.
13. Using a sharp knife, score the top of the pie into squares or diamonds, being careful not to cut all the way through the bottom layers.
14. Bake the kolokithopita in the preheated oven for 45-50 minutes, or until the phyllo is golden brown and crispy.
15. Remove from the oven and let the pie cool for a few minutes before slicing and serving.

Enjoy your delicious kolokithopita warm or at room temperature, as a main dish or appetizer. It pairs wonderfully with a fresh Greek salad or tzatziki sauce!

Greek-style Roasted Vegetables

Ingredients:

- 2 medium potatoes, peeled and cut into chunks
- 2 medium carrots, peeled and cut into chunks
- 1 red bell pepper, seeded and cut into chunks
- 1 yellow bell pepper, seeded and cut into chunks
- 1 green bell pepper, seeded and cut into chunks
- 1 red onion, cut into wedges
- 1 zucchini, sliced
- 1 small eggplant, cubed
- 4 cloves garlic, minced
- 3 tablespoons olive oil
- 1 tablespoon fresh lemon juice
- 1 teaspoon dried oregano
- 1 teaspoon dried thyme
- 1 teaspoon dried rosemary
- Salt and pepper to taste
- Lemon wedges and fresh parsley for garnish (optional)

Instructions:

1. Preheat your oven to 400°F (200°C).
2. In a large mixing bowl, combine the potatoes, carrots, bell peppers, red onion, zucchini, and eggplant.
3. In a small bowl, whisk together the minced garlic, olive oil, lemon juice, dried oregano, dried thyme, dried rosemary, salt, and pepper.
4. Pour the olive oil mixture over the vegetables in the large mixing bowl. Toss until the vegetables are evenly coated with the seasoning mixture.
5. Spread the seasoned vegetables out in a single layer on a large baking sheet lined with parchment paper or aluminum foil.
6. Roast the vegetables in the preheated oven for 30-35 minutes, or until they are tender and lightly browned, stirring halfway through the cooking time for even browning.
7. Once the vegetables are roasted to your liking, remove them from the oven and transfer them to a serving dish.
8. Garnish the roasted vegetables with fresh parsley and lemon wedges, if desired.

9. Serve the Greek-style roasted vegetables as a side dish or as a main course with crusty bread or over cooked grains like quinoa or couscous.

Enjoy the delicious flavors of these Greek-style roasted vegetables, packed with Mediterranean herbs and spices!

Pita Bread with Greek Yogurt and Cucumber

Ingredients:

- 2 pita bread rounds
- 1 cup Greek yogurt
- 1/2 cucumber, peeled and grated
- 1 clove garlic, minced
- 1 tablespoon fresh lemon juice
- 1 tablespoon extra virgin olive oil
- 1 tablespoon chopped fresh dill (optional)
- Salt and pepper to taste

Instructions:

1. Start by making the tzatziki sauce. In a mixing bowl, combine the Greek yogurt, grated cucumber, minced garlic, lemon juice, olive oil, chopped dill (if using), salt, and pepper. Stir until well combined. Taste and adjust seasoning if needed. Refrigerate the tzatziki sauce while you prepare the pita bread.
2. Preheat a grill or grill pan over medium heat. If you don't have a grill, you can also use a toaster or oven to warm the pita bread.
3. Lightly brush both sides of the pita bread rounds with olive oil.
4. Place the pita bread on the grill or grill pan and cook for 1-2 minutes on each side, or until lightly toasted and grill marks appear.
5. Once the pita bread is toasted, remove it from the grill and let it cool slightly.
6. Cut each pita bread round in half to create pockets.
7. Stuff each pita pocket with a generous amount of the prepared tzatziki sauce.
8. Serve the tzatziki-filled pita bread immediately as a light meal or snack.

Enjoy the refreshing combination of creamy tzatziki sauce with crunchy cucumber in warm, toasted pita bread! It's perfect for a quick and satisfying bite.

Grilled Calamari

Ingredients:

- 1 lb (450g) cleaned squid tubes and tentacles
- 2-3 tablespoons olive oil
- 2 cloves garlic, minced
- Zest and juice of 1 lemon
- 1 teaspoon dried oregano
- Salt and pepper to taste
- Lemon wedges and fresh parsley for garnish

Instructions:

1. Start by preparing the squid. Rinse the squid under cold water and pat it dry with paper towels. If the squid tubes are whole, slice them open lengthwise so they lay flat.
2. In a bowl, whisk together the olive oil, minced garlic, lemon zest, lemon juice, dried oregano, salt, and pepper to make the marinade.
3. Place the cleaned squid in a shallow dish or resealable plastic bag, and pour the marinade over it. Make sure the squid is evenly coated with the marinade. Let it marinate for about 15-30 minutes at room temperature, or longer in the refrigerator if you have time.
4. Preheat your grill to medium-high heat. If you're using a charcoal grill, make sure the coals are hot and glowing.
5. Remove the squid from the marinade and shake off any excess. Discard the marinade.
6. Place the squid on the preheated grill. Cook for about 2-3 minutes per side, or until the squid is opaque and grill marks appear. Be careful not to overcook the squid, as it can become tough and rubbery.
7. Once the squid is cooked, remove it from the grill and transfer it to a serving platter.
8. Garnish the grilled calamari with fresh parsley and lemon wedges.
9. Serve the grilled calamari hot as an appetizer or main dish, alongside your favorite dipping sauce or a squeeze of fresh lemon juice.

Enjoy the delicious flavor and tender texture of grilled calamari, a perfect dish for seafood lovers!

Greek-style Grilled Eggplant

Ingredients:

- 2 large eggplants
- Salt
- Olive oil
- 2 cloves garlic, minced
- 2 tablespoons chopped fresh parsley
- 1 tablespoon chopped fresh mint (optional)
- Juice of 1 lemon
- Crumbled feta cheese (optional, for serving)
- Lemon wedges (for serving)

Instructions:

1. Start by preparing the eggplants. Trim off the stem ends, then slice the eggplants lengthwise into 1/4-inch thick slices.
2. Lay the eggplant slices on a baking sheet or large plate, and sprinkle both sides generously with salt. Let them sit for about 30 minutes. This helps to draw out any bitterness from the eggplants.
3. After 30 minutes, rinse the eggplant slices under cold water to remove the excess salt. Pat them dry with paper towels.
4. Preheat your grill to medium-high heat.
5. Brush both sides of the eggplant slices with olive oil. You can use a pastry brush or simply drizzle the olive oil over the slices and rub it in with your hands.
6. Place the eggplant slices on the preheated grill. Cook for about 3-4 minutes per side, or until they are tender and have nice grill marks. Be sure to monitor them closely to prevent burning.
7. While the eggplant is grilling, prepare the dressing. In a small bowl, combine the minced garlic, chopped parsley, chopped mint (if using), and lemon juice. Mix well.
8. Once the eggplant slices are done grilling, transfer them to a serving platter.
9. Drizzle the garlic and herb dressing over the grilled eggplant slices.
10. If desired, sprinkle crumbled feta cheese over the top of the grilled eggplant.
11. Serve the Greek-style grilled eggplant hot, with lemon wedges on the side for squeezing over the top.

Enjoy the delicious flavors of tender grilled eggplant with garlic, herbs, and tangy lemon juice, a perfect addition to any Mediterranean-inspired meal!

Loukoumades (Greek Honey Puffs)

Ingredients:

For the Dough:

- 1 package (2 1/4 teaspoons) active dry yeast
- 1 cup lukewarm water
- 3 cups all-purpose flour
- 1/2 teaspoon salt
- Vegetable oil for frying

For Serving:

- Honey
- Ground cinnamon
- Chopped walnuts (optional)

Instructions:

1. In a small bowl, dissolve the active dry yeast in lukewarm water. Let it sit for about 5 minutes until it becomes frothy.
2. In a large mixing bowl, combine the flour and salt. Make a well in the center and pour in the yeast mixture. Stir until a sticky dough forms.
3. Cover the bowl with a clean kitchen towel and let the dough rise in a warm place for about 1-2 hours, or until it doubles in size.
4. Heat vegetable oil in a deep fryer or large pot to 350°F (175°C).
5. Once the dough has risen, use a spoon or small ice cream scoop to drop small portions of dough into the hot oil. Be careful not to overcrowd the pot. Fry the loukoumades in batches, turning occasionally, until they are golden brown and puffed up, about 2-3 minutes.
6. Use a slotted spoon to remove the loukoumades from the oil and transfer them to a plate lined with paper towels to drain excess oil.
7. While the loukoumades are still warm, drizzle them generously with honey and sprinkle with ground cinnamon. You can also add chopped walnuts for extra flavor and crunch.
8. Serve the loukoumades immediately, while they are still warm and crispy.

Enjoy the heavenly taste of homemade loukoumades, a perfect indulgence for any occasion!